Mammals of Long Ago

By Allan Fowler

Consultants
Linda Cornwell, Coordinator of School Quality
and Professional Improvement
Indiana State Teachers Association

Janann V. Jenner, Ph.D.

38106000005516

Children's Press®
A Division of Grolier Publishing
New York   London   Hong Kong   Sydney
Danbury, Connecticut

Visit Children's Press® on the Internet at:
http://publishing.grolier.com

Designer: Herman Adler Design Group
Photo Researcher: Caroline Anderson

The mammals shown on the cover lived more than 10,000 years ago
and are closely related to elephants. What are these creatures called?
Read on to find out.

Library of Congress Cataloging-in-Publication Data

Fowler, Allan.
    Mammals of long ago / by Allan Fowler.
        p. cm. — (Rookie read-about science)
    Includes index.
    Summary: A brief introduction to a number of extinct mammals that
lived from the time of the dinosaurs to the late Ice Age.
    ISBN 0-516-21209-5 (lib. bdg.)   0-516-27090-7 (pbk.)
    1. Mammals, Fossils—Juvenile literature. [1. Mammals, Fossil.]
QE881.F68   2000
569—dc21   98-26397
                                                              CIP
                                                              AC

©2000 Children's Press®
A Division of Grolier Publishing Co., Inc.
All rights reserved. Published simultaneously in Canada.
Printed in the United States of America.
1 2 3 4 5 6 7 8 9 10 R 09 08 07 06 05 04 03 02 01 00

Diplodocus

Millions of years ago,
dinosaurs lived on Earth.

Tyrannosaurus rex

These giant reptiles
ruled the land, the sea,
and the air.

Pteranodons flew through the air. *Plesiosaurus* swam in the sea.

Parasaurolophus

Today there are no dinosaurs left. When a group of animals is gone forever, we say it is extinct.

A group of animals becomes extinct when the last animal dies.

When the dinosaurs died,
mammals began to take
over Earth.

All mammals have hair
and feed their young
mother's milk.

Puppies drink mother's milk.

Can you name some mammals?

Lion

Humpback whale

Lions, dogs, whales, and
bats are all mammals.
People are mammals, too.

Long ago, many strange
mammals lived on Earth.
These mammals are
extinct now.

Some of them looked
a lot like animals that
are alive today.

This painting shows some animals that lived in California about 10,000 years ago.

Saber-toothed cat

The saber-toothed cat had
huge, pointed teeth and
was the size of a tiger.

Bengal tiger

Mesohippus   Horse

16

The first horses were much smaller than the horses that live today. *Mesohippus* (MEZ-o-hip-is) had three toes on each foot. How many toes does a modern horse have?

Giant ground sloths were huge animals that lived in North America. Today, sloths live only in Central America.

Giant ground sloth

Brown-thumbed three-toed sloth

They are about the
same size as a pet cat.

How was an early
rhinoceros named
Trigonias (tre-GOUN-i-as)
different from the
rhinos that live today?

It had no horns.

Trigonias

Black rhinoceros

21

MAMMOTH
PLEISTOCENE
PERIOD
1½ million years ago
plant eater
Length 22 feet Ht. 15 feet

Mammoth

Mammoths looked like elephants with heavy, shaggy coats. They had long tusks that curved back.

African elephant

Mastodons looked like
elephants, too. They had
tusks that curved up.

Mastodon

Cave painting in France

Scientists know that early people lived at the same time as saber-toothed cats, early horses, and mammoths.

The early people painted these mammals on the walls of caves.

There are many kinds
of mammals alive today.

But the number of
extinct mammals is
much, much greater.

29

Words You Know

dinosaur

giant ground sloths

mammal

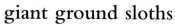

mammoth

mastodon

Mesohippus

saber-toothed cat

Trigonias

31

Index

About the Author

Allan Fowler is a freelance writer with a background in advertising.
Born in New York, he now lives in Chicago and enjoys traveling.

Photo Credits

©: Animals Animals: 16 right (Gerard Lacz); George C. Page Museum: 13; Peter
Arnold Inc.: 22, 29 top right, 30 bottom right (Stephen J. Krassemann); Photo
Researchers: 11 (François Gohier), 21 bottom (Renee Lynn), 14, 29 bottom left,
31 bottom left (Tom McHugh); Superstock, Inc.: 3, 4, 5, 6, 9, 26, 30 top left,
30 bottom left; Tony Stone Images: 10 (Daniel J. Cox); Visuals Unlimited:
16 left, 29 background, 31 top right, 19 (Larry Kimball), 23 (Leonard Lee Rue III),
15 (Kjell B. Sandved), cover, 18, 21 top, 25, 29 top left, 29 center right, 29 bottom
right, 30 top right, 31 top left, 31 bottom right (Science VU).